THE STORY OF JAIN AND PARSI FOOD

DR ANSHUMALI PANDEY

Contents

ONE
JAIN FOOD

In the 6th century BC many people were beginning to oppose the hierarchical organisation and formalised rituals of Hinduism, the dominant religion in India. The word Jain is derived from Jina, which means the one victorious over the self and the external world. The Jinas are regarded more respect than the Gods. They include the 24 Tirthankaras or ford – finders (holy men), the last Tirthankara Mahavira (599 – 527 BC) is the founder of Jainism. After Mahavira's death, two major sects were formed: the 'Svetambara' and the 'Digambaras'. This schism was caused due to a disagreement regarding the monastery discipline: the Schvetambaras believed that the monks and nuns should wear white robes, but the Digambaras believed that just like Mahavira the monks should wander naked and that a female cannot be a nun because she cannot attain liberation. This led the Schvetambaras to exclude the Digambaras from the orthodox Jain council. The Jain community remains very isolated from other communities. Nevertheless, they are one of the wealthiest communities in India and most influential in the finance and business sectors.

TWO

FEATURES OF THE JAIN CUISINE

It naturally follows then that strict followers of the religion have a thick list of dos and donts. The most obvious ones include all kinds of meat, avian life (including eggs), and seafood. Root vegetables, and anything that grows below the ground (including onion, garlic, potatoes, carrots) is also verboten, since in the process of digging them up, insects living underground may be harmed. Fermented foods using live yeast or rennet is not allowed. Alcohol is shunned because fermentation is involved, and because it may cloud one's judgment, leading to violence. Eating after dark is frowned upon. And in a heartening, rallying cry to those protesting the excesses of the industrial dairy industry, some Jains will only accept milk and other dairy products if they know that the cows and buffaloes are being well treated. They also avoid multi – seeded fruits and vegetables, such as figs and eggplants. The promise of life inherent in such produce is too important to be sacrificed to the lust of the palate. Honey is forbidden food, since removing it from the comb would involve the death of bees. Even betel leaves, the pan – Indian after dinner chaser, are out of bounds, since they are always smeared with a lime paste to which ground up shells are often added. As for the thin silver foil that is used as a decorative coating for cardamom seeds or sweets, Jains won't touch it, since the metal has to be beaten to papery thinness between layers of soft leather, or worse, the intestines of cows.

During their eight – day fast of Paryushan, which is undertaken during the monsoon season, while the holiest undertake a complete fast (only boiled water is allowed), there are restrictions placed on others as well. According to her, "Greens, normally relished, are forbidden at this time, in a symbolic acknowledgement that the monsoon rains bring to life a host of insects that might cling to the leaves. Jains don't even garnish their khandvis and dhoklas with fresh coriander leaves". During Paryushan, Jain culinary creativity reaches its zenith, through an array of gravied and dry dishes that are made without vegetables (although certain sections of the Jain community do eat capsicum and such veggies). For instance, Papad Churi (spiced, crumbled papad eaten as a snack); Panchmela Dal (five types of dal cooked together); spicy and sour mung pani; Choonbadi (gram flour dumplings, cooked in curd); Sorghum Rotis; Mogar Sabzi (moong dal); Bapadi Rotli (ghee – soaked layers of roti); steamed mung cakes and chickpea cakes; all washed down with a light tea made from Kariyatu, a bitter herb. Traditionally cooking or eating at night was discouraged because insects are attracted to the lamps or fire at night. Strict Jains take the vow (called anastamita or anthau) of not eating after sunset. Strict Jains do not consume food which has been stored overnight, as it possesses a higher concentration of micro – organisms (for example, bacteria yeast etc) as compared to food prepared and consumed the same day. Hence, they do not consume yogurt or dhokla & idli batter unless they've been freshly set on the same day. Jains do not consume fermented foods (beer, wine and other alcohols) to avoid killing of a large number of microorganisms associated with the fermenting process. During some specific fasting periods in the Jain religious "Panchang" calendar, Jains refrain from consuming any green coloured vegetables (which have chlorophyll pigment) such as okra, leafy vegetables, etc. In spite of all the restrictions facing them, the Jains have conjured up an absolutely delightful cuisine, making the most of what is available to them, whether in Gujarat or Rajasthan or Maharashtra. With tremendous ingenuity, legumes, beans, rice, wheat and permitted fruits and vegetables, they are transformed into delicious dishes, for instance, Jain Pao Bhaji or pizza (served without onions etc), when far more unique and delicious cooking is available.For example, Jains have learnt to cook with fruits. From the guava, they make a most delicious Peru nu Shak (guava sabzi). Soaked mango seeds are whipped into Kadhis, and the mango peels are consigned into yoghurt gravies. Atta is effortlessly converted to puddings, by way of RECIPES like Atte ka Halwa, and Gol Papdi (a sweet made from ghee, atta and jaggery). Then there is also Lapsee (made from dalia), and mithi (sweet) khichdi.

THREE
POPULAR JAIN FOODS

- **Bajri Na Dhebra**: A poori like dish that carries with it a flavor of spice and texture of crunch that gives a food lover an exotic eating experience. The deep fried dish is a special occasional dish to treat guests or a super dish for a chilly cold winter evening or a rainy evening alongside some chai!
- **Khatta Dhokla**: White Dhokla recipe is made using rice, yoghurt and split black gram. It is popularly known as Gujarati Khatta Dhokla since it has a signature sour taste which is what makes so many people a fan of it. Also called *Irda*
- **Amrood Ni Kari**: or guava curry is an unusual Rajasthani curry made using just ripened guava in a curd based gravy.
- **Avalakki** Bella Usuli: Thin poha that is tossed in coarsly ground spices, coconut, a hint of jaggary and simple tempering.
- **Banana Chutney**: Chutney made from ripe bananas.

- **Bhakri**: It is a round flat unleavened bread often buscuit like, flavoured with ghee and cumin sedds. All time favourite teatime snacks.
- **Cabbage Paratha**: Crunchy oparathas with filling of cabbage and cheese, green chillies and green coriander.
- **Dal Makhani**: A creamy dal filled with of rajma beans and urad dal and delicately flavoured with spices and ginger made with no onion and no garlic. Serve with any indian bread or rice for a comforting meal.
- **Dalia khichdi**: It is made from broken wheat, moong dal (yellow lentil) and vegetables. The consistency of daliya khichdi is very soft which makes it easy for kids to swallow and is also a perfect comfort food, more so during winters.
- **Dhokla**: It is made with a fermented batter derived from rice and split chickpeas. Dhokla can be eaten for breakfast, as a main course, as a side dish, or as a snack.
- **Fafda**: A popular snacks made from the Chana Flour and goes well with Jalebis.
- **Kapuriya**: It is an instant version of dhokla.
- **Karela chutney**: sweet chutney made with bitter gourd
- **Khichu**: Khichu or Khichiyu is a dough for making papad, however, owing to its taste it is also consumed as Farsan (snack/side dish). It is made from rice flour in which cumin seeds and other seasonings are added.
- **Lauki Burfi**: This burfi recipe is prepared with bottle gourd, full cream milk, khoya, ghee, green cardamom and a pinch of salt.
- **Meethe Chawal**: Rice cooked with saffron, nuts, sugar and elaichi flavor and served hot.
- **Mixed Vegetable Handvo**: It is a vegetable dish which is based on gram flour (called Besan in Hindi and Urdu) and contains vegetables like peas, cabbage, and also

includes Garam masala. It is often eaten with Pickle or tea.

- **Pappu charu**: Soup made of Arhar dal. Pappu means dal and charu term is used for thin, tangy consistency of extract or soup.
- **Puruppu payasam**: It is called moong dal kheer or payasam. This payasam is more popular in between jains from Kerala and Tamilnadu.
- **Sabudana chewda**: Sabudana are fried till crispy and puffy, then mixed with nuts, salt, pepper, sugar and green chilies. This makes good snack for navratri vrat or any other Jain festival of snacks.
- **Sookhi Moong Dal**: Moong dal cooked with urmeric powder, chilli powder and garam masala and added lime juice.

FOUR

JAIN FESTIVALS AND CELEBRATIONS

Paryushan Mahaparva – Paryushana Parva is one of the most important festival for Jains. Paryusana is formed by two words meaning 'a year' and 'a coming back'. This festival comes in the months of Shravana and Bhadra (August or September). Svetambara Jains celebrate it for eight – days while Digambara Jains celebrate it for ten days. It is also known as Das Lakshana Parva. It is a festival of repentance and forgiveness. Many Jains fast and carry out different religious activities. Jain monks stop walking during chaturmas and reside at one place where they lecture on various religious subjects during paryushana. This festival is believed to remove accumulated karma of the previous year and develop control over new accumulating new karma, by following Jain austerities and other rituals. There are regular rituals at the Jain temples. Discourses of Kalpa Sutra are given by monks. Kalpa Sutra describes life of Mahavira and other Tirthankaras. On the third day, procession of Kalpa Sutra is carried out. On the fifth day, auspicious dreams of Trishala, mother of Mahavira are demonstrated and after that birth of Mahavira is celebrated. The tenth day of festival is called Anant Chaurdsashi. Anant Chaturdashi is the day when Lord Vasupujya attained moksha (nirvan). Usually, a procession is taken out by Jains on this day. Kshamavani is generally observed a day after Anant Chaturdashi by digambaras, while the shwetambaras observe it after the 8th ie the last day of their paryushan (last day is called samvatsari). On Kshamavani, Jains ask for forgiveness from everybody for any acts during the previous year which may have hurt them.

Navpad Oli – Jain observes Festival of Navpad oli, that last for nine days, twice a year. The first one falls in the bright fortnight of Ashwina month (September/October) and the second during the bright fortnight of Chaitra month (March/April).Ayambil Tap is a kind of fast during which boiled grains without salt is partaken only once during the day. Ayambil Tap is observed to offer salutations to the nine Supreme posts in the Universe. The nine Supreme posts are: Arihant, Siddha, Acharya, Upadhyaya, Sadhu, Samyag Darshan, Samyag Gyan, Samyag Charitra and Samyag Tapa. Nava means nine and Pad means posts. Thus a festival which is celebrated to salute the nine supreme posts is known as Navpad Oli.

Mahaveer Jayanti – Mahavira's birthday is on the 13th day of the month of Caitra in the Indian calendar, which falls in late March or early April. Mahavira's auspicious birth (kalnayaka) is observed by both Jain sects, the Digambaras ('sky clad' or naked) and Svetambaras ('white clad' or clothed).and in India images of Mahavira are paraded in the streets with much pomp and celebration.

Bhai Beej – The festival day for brothers.When Raja Nandivardhan, the brother of Shraman Bhagawan Mahavir was steeped in sorrow and anguish on account of the latter's nirvan (attainment of Mukti) his sister, Sudarshana took him to her house and comforted him. This happened on the second day of the fortnight of the waxing moon, in Kartik. This day is observed as Bhai Beej. This festival is like Raksha Bandhan. On the day of Rakshabandhan, the sister goes to the brother and ties the Raksha; but on this day, the sister invites her brother to her house to felicitate him.

Jnan Panchami – Jnan Panchami is the name given to the celebration that takes place on the 5th day of the fortnight of the waxing moon in Kartik (the 5th day after Diwali). This day has been fixed for the worship of pure knowledge; and on this day, by way of worshipping knowledge, fasting, taking Paushadh, devavandan (offering veneration to Gods). Holy recitation, meditation, Pratikraman etc., are carried out. Moreover the books preserved in the religious libraries are cleansed and worshiped.

Ashadh Chaturdasi – The sacred commencement of Chaturmas takes place on the 14th day of the fortnight of the waxing moon, in the month of Ashad. The Jain Sadhus and Sadhvis remain where they happen to be on that day until the 14th day of Kartik Shukla. They have to stay there. During these four months among the Jains, many austerities like renunciation, tapasya, undertaking of religious ceremonies, etc., are organized. Even in respect of eating and drinking during these days, some rules have been prescribed.

Maun Agiyara – or Ekadashi marks Kalyanaka of many Tirthankaras. It is celebrated on 11th day of Magshar month of Jain calendar (October/November). This is an important day for Jains on which they observe total silence – Maun and carry outsuch austerities as Paushadh vrat, fasting, worshipping of gods, meditation etc. This is the day on which the great events relating to the one hundred and fifty Jineswaras are celebrated by means of holy recitation.

Varshi Tapa or Akshaya Tritiya – On this day, first Jain Tirthankara Rishabha or Lord Adinath, completed austerity —Paranal after fasting continuously for 13 months and 13 days. People who perform Varshi Tapa, complete the fasting by taking sugarcane juice. Some people also offer community lunch to celebrate the completion of Varshi Tapa.

Maha-mastak-abhisheka – This festival is celebrated once in twelve years in Shravanabelagola, Karnataka. This festival is celebrated once in twelve years in Shravanabelagola, Karnataka. The18 meters high statue of Lord Bahubali is worshipped by thousands of devotees who assemble from all over. The statue is bathed in milk, honey, saffron, scents, flowers, and many other rich religious ingredients of the world. The 18 meters high statue is bathed in milk, honey, saffron, scents, flowers, and many other rich religious ingredients of the world. They also sprinkle sandalwood, turmeric, and vermilion on the statue. The Lord is offered flower petals, precious gems and gold and silver coins. According to the Jainism this worship is very fruitful and for the upliftment of the soul.

FIVE

IMPORTANT DISHES OF JAIN CUISINE

Handvo

Ingredients

- Green peas boiled–½ cup
- Yogurt warm–½ cup
- Green capsicum finely chopped–1 small
- Sweet Corn boiled–2 tablespoons
- handvo flour– 1½ cups
- Bottle gourd (lauki/doodhi) peeled and grated–½ small
- Green chillies finely chopped–2
- Turmeric powder– ¼ teaspoon
- Red chilli powder – 1 teaspoon
- Sugar– 1 teaspoon
- Salt – taste

- Oil – for cooking
- Fruit salt– 1 teaspoon
- Mustard seeds– 2 teaspoons
- White sesame seeds– 4 teaspoons

Method

- Combine handvo flour and yogurt in a bowl. Add water as required and whisk well into a thick smooth batter.
- Add green peas, bottle gourd, capsicum, corn and green chillies and mix well. Add turmeric powder, red chilli powder, sugar and salt and mix well. Add little water and mix well.
- Heat some oil in a non – stick pan.
- Add fruit salt to the batter and mix well.
- Add ½ teaspoon mustard seeds and 1 teaspoon sesame seeds in the pan and when the seeds start to splutter, pour a ladleful of batter on it and spread into a 1 inch thick large disc. Cover and cook on the underside for 5 – 10 minutes.
- Flip, drizzle some more oil all around, cover and cook on the other side for 3 – 4 minutes. Similarly prepare the rest of the handvos.
- Cut into wedges and serve hot.

Dhokla

Ingredients

- Semolina–1cup

- Sour curd – 1 cup
- Water – 1 cup
- Salt – to Taste
- Chopped coriander – ½ cup
- Chopped green chillies –2
- Oil – 1 tbsp
- Fruit Salt (Eno) – ½ tsp

For Seasoning

- Oil – 1tsp
- Mustard seeds – 1tsp
- Cumin seeds – 1 tsp
- Green chilly (slit) – 1
- Sesame seeds – tsp

Method

- Mix semolina with yoghurt, add salt, green chilli, coriander, oil and water to make a smooth batter (add water if needed to bring it to a consistency of condensed milk). Keep it for 15 – 20 mins.
- Meantime grease the steel trays of dhokla maker with oil. Boil around an inch of water in dhokla maker.
- Add Eno to the above mix, stir and immediately add mix to the greased trays.
- Sprinkle red chilli powder or black pepper powder on the mix (optional).
- Steam on medium flame for 10 – 12 mins.
- Check with toothpick if dhokla is steamed (toothpick should come out clean).
- Heat oil in a pan, add mustard seeds, cumin seeds, green chilli, sesame seeds. Sprinkle chopped coriander on

steamed dhoklas and pour the seasoning on it.
- Serve hot with green chutney or tomato ketchup.

Dal Makhani

Ingredients

- Whole Black Grams soaked overnight – 3/4 cup
- Red Kidney Beans soaked overnight – 2 tbsp
- Salt – to taste
- Butter – 4 tablespoons
- Cumin seeds – 1 teaspoon
- Green chillies slit – 2
- Cinnamon 1 inch stick
- Green cardamoms – 3
- Red chilli powder – 1 tsp
- Turmeric powder 1/4 tsp
- Tomatoes pureed – 3 large
- Fresh cream – 3/4 cup
- Fresh coriander leaves chopped – 2 tbsp

Method

- Combine sabut urad and rajma in a pressure cooker. Add two cups of water and salt.
- Pressure cook till four to five whistles or till they are completely cooked and soft. Open the lid when the pressure has reduced and whisk till they almost completely mashed.
- Heat three tablespoons butter in a deep pan and add cumin seeds.

- When they begin to change colour, add green chillies, cinnamon, cloves and green cardamoms and sauté till fragrant.
- Add red chilli powder, turmeric powder, dry ginger powder and tomato puree and sauté on medium heat till the oil begins to separate from the masala.
- Add the dal mixture, one cup of water and stir to mix well.
- Adjust salt and simmer for ten minutes or till the required consistency is reached.
- Add cream and mix well. Serve hot garnished with coriander leaves and topped with the remaining butter.

Khatta Dhokla

Ingredients

- Rice – 2cups
- Skinless Black Gram (Urid dal) – 1cup
- Sour Curd – 1/2 cup
- Fresh cream – 1 tbsp
- Salt – to taste
- Green Chillies (finely chopped) – 2 – 3
- Red Chilli Powder/Black Pepper Powder – ½ tsp
- Fruit salt(Eno) – 1tsp

Method

- Dry grind rice and urid dal in a mixer to a coarse powder.

- Warm curd and add to rice and urid dal flour.
- Add warm water and mix everything to a thick paste.
- Allow the mixture to ferment for 3 – 4 hours.
- Add grren chillies, fresh cream and salt to fermented mixture.
- Grease a metal thali with oil and keep it ready to steam.
- Add eno to the mixture and mix it well.
- Pour the batter in greased thali (about half filled), sprinkle red chilli powder/black pepper powder and steam it for 10 minutes.
- Cut Khatta dhokla into diamond pieces and serve with oil and green chutney.

<u>Meethe Chawal</u>

Ingredients

- Rice – 2 cup
- Green cardamom – 5
- Sugar – as required
- Raisins – 1 tbsp
- Chopped almonds – ½ cup
- Edible food color – 1 tsp
- Vegetable oil – 1 tbsp
- Heavy cream – 1 ½ tbsp
- Chopped walnuts – ½ cup
- Orange zest – 1 tsp

Method

- To prepare this dessert recipe, add rice in a medium sized bowl and wash 3 – 4 times to remove the dust

particles.
- Then, pour water to the bowl and cover it using a foil paper or cloth.
- Soak the rice for about an hour.
- Next, put a deep – bottomed pan on medium flame and boil water in it.
- After a boil, add orange food colour in the water along with half the quantity of cardamom pods, and switch off the burner.
- Then, put a medium sized kadhai over medium flame and heat vegetable oil in it.
- When the oil is hot enough, saute the remaining cardamom pods for about a minute.
- Drain the extra water from the soaked rice and add them to the kadhai along with sugar as per your taste and coloured water.
- Stir to mix once and cover the kadhai using a lid and cook for 5 – 7 minutes.
- Then, add orange zest, almonds, walnuts, raisins along with fresh cream to the kadhai and mix once again.
- Remove the kadhai from the burner.
- When the rice are done, transfer in a bowl and serve hot.

Lauki Burfi

Ingredients

- Grated,peeled bottle gourd – 4 cup
- Khoya – 125 gm
- Ghee – 1 tbsp
- Sugar – ¼ cup
- Full cream milk – ½ litre

- Powdered green cardamom – 1 tsp
- Salt – 1 pinch

For garnishing

- Chopped almonds – as required
- Chopped pistachios – as required

Method

- To prepare this amazingly delicious dessert recipe, put a deep – bottomed and non – stick pan on medium flame and add milk in it.
- Bring the milk to a boil and then add grated bottle guard. Stir to mix well and let it simmer for about 10 – 15 minutes.
- Now, add sugar in the pan and give a nice stir, cook well till the milk is absorbed by the bottle gourd and thickens in consistency.
- Afterwards, add khoya in the pan along with ghee, and cardamom powder. Stir to mix once again.
- Meanwhile, take a large plate and grease with a little ghee. Once the milk is absorbed completely, turn off the burner and transfer the prepared halwa into the plate.
- Spread it evenly and garnish with chopped pistachio and almonds. Keep it aside to cool at room temperature.
- Once the halwa is cool enough, refrigerate it for 4 – 5 hours to set the burfi.
- Take out after some time and cut into desired shapes and sizes.
- Serve immediately. (Note: You can also store it in refrigerator in an air – tight container.)

SIX

PARSI FOODS

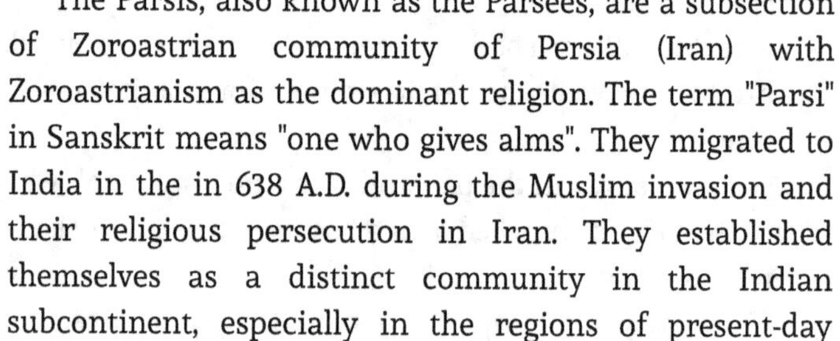

The Parsis, also known as the Parsees, are a subsection of Zoroastrian community of Persia (Iran) with Zoroastrianism as the dominant religion. The term "Parsi" in Sanskrit means "one who gives alms". They migrated to India in the in 638 A.D. during the Muslim invasion and their religious persecution in Iran. They established themselves as a distinct community in the Indian subcontinent, especially in the regions of present-day Maharashtra and Gujarat. The **"Qissa-i Sanjan"**, Story of Sanjan is the only existing account of the early years of Parsi settlers on the Indian subcontinent. It accounts the first settlement of Parsis in Sanjan of the present day Gujrat.

They first settled in the Indian Province of Gujarat under Raja Jadi Rana, the king and they slowly migrated to the different cosmopolitan cities of India. Under British rule, the Parsis adopted British clothing and were actively involved in promoting education for girls and the abolition of child marriage. Today it is the smallest community of the world consisting of about 75,000 people. Over the decades they managed to develop a unique cuisine of their own which was a perfect mixture Maharashtrian, Gujarati and British flavours adding to India's rich culinary heritage. Dishes reveal traces of the past in the fondness for nuts, dry fruit and sweet flavours while the Indian influence is the addition of onions, garlic and ginger which make the food savoury but not spicy.

SEVEN

FEATURES OF THE PARSI CUISINE

They also adopted part of the local cuisine but maintained their distinctive culture. Parsi food is a mix of vegetarian Gujarati cuisine and non – vegetarian Iranian cuisine. Since Parsi first settled in Sajjan, in Gujarat which is the coastal area. Their cuisine is influence by fish. Coconut is the ingredient most of the Parsi food. In their cuisine herbs are frequently used along with fruits such as plums, apricot and raisins. The main Persian cuisines are rice with meat, lamb or fish and some onion, vegetables, nuts and herbs. To achieve balanced taste, characteristic Persian flavoring such as saffron is used. Cinnamon, parsley and dried lime are mixed delicately and used in special dishes. Since they settled in India they started using Garlic, Ginger, Red chilles and tamarind in their cuisine.

- The Parsi curry is composed of coconut and spices. Coconut, fish, and rice are considered to be the way of life and any Parsi feast is incomplete without the inclusion of these three. Parsis are connoisseurs of non – vegetarian food, and drink.
- Almost all the vegetable dishes made from okra, tomatoes or potatoes will have eggs on top.
- Because of the Iranian roots, the stewing of vegetables, lentils and meat together in Parsi cuisine similar to the practice in Iranian cuisine. The meat is combined with vegetables such as okra, green peas and nuts.
- The use of the flavour of rose water is again an Iranian influence on the Parsi cuisine.
- The halwas and the murabbas made under this cuisine is also the Iran effect on the cuisine.
- The Parsi preference for egg (eeda) has led to the making of certain egg specialities such as kera per eeda (eggs cooked on banana) and akuri (masala scrambled eggs)
- The fat medium preferred in the cuisine is ghee. Mustard oil and peanut oil also finds common use. The use of ginger and garlic is also very prominent in the Parsi cuisine.
- Garnishing of the dishes with fine straw potatoes (Sali) is common.
- Vinegar and sugar– Many Parsi dishes use this unique balance of acid and sweetness called _khattu mithu.' A popular Parsi tomato – based curry is the
- 'Patio'; made using this method. The turkey mince (Kheemo) in this recipe is another example of how these two elements work together in a dish.
- The large selection of pickles and chutneys are adapted from the western coasts of India such as Konkan and Maharashtra.

- Snacks such as bhakra (deep fried sweet dough), batasa (flour and butter tea biscuits) etc are an influence of the Gujrati cuisine on that of the Parsi cuisine. Other snacks include dar ni pori (sweetened lentils stuffed in a light pastry) and khaman na lavda (dumplings stuffed with sweetened coconut).

- Balance of dried fruits, fresh fruits and nuts– Dried fruit like apricots and raisins, nuts like pistachio and almond appears commonly in Parsi dishes. And it is not uncommon to find fresh fruits like pomegranate and bananas in the food. A boneless lamb preparation using apricots (Jardaloo Sali Boti) is a hot favourite.

- Sweet dishes also are an area of importance in this cuisine. Few famous desserts of the Parsi cuisine resembles apuff pastry and this has been probably influenced by certain desserts made in Turkey and the Middle East that use an ingredient called phyllo to make desserts such as baklava.

- Ghau nu doodh is wheat soaked in water for about two days, changing the water everyday. The soaked wheat is then ground to a paste and hung in a cloth. The dripping are collected and when dried, they are broken or ground and then stored until further use. It is used to prepare many puddings such as soova pak (reduced milk pudding flavoured with dill and deep fried ghau nu doodh and nuts).

- In Parsi cooking, people do not prefer to roast too many spices as they believe in the preserving the nutrition and the rich flavour of the condiments. Some special ingredients used in the cuisine apart from the normal ones include: Apricots (jardaloo), date palm (Galeli), charoli, etc.

- In Parsi tradition, the dinner is considered the main meal of the day. Parsi meal style:
- Their breakfast consists of eggs, bread and tea.
- The basic feature of a Parsi lunch is rice, eaten with lentils, meat, fish or vegetable curry. Curry is normally coconut based.
- Dinner is considered the main meal of the day and is a combination of eggs, fish, meat and poultry eaten with rice and finished with fruits and nuts. Potatoes or other vegetablecurries along with Kachumber (onion salad) accompanies most meals.

EIGHT

EQUIPMENT AND UTENSILS USED IN THE PARSI CUISINE

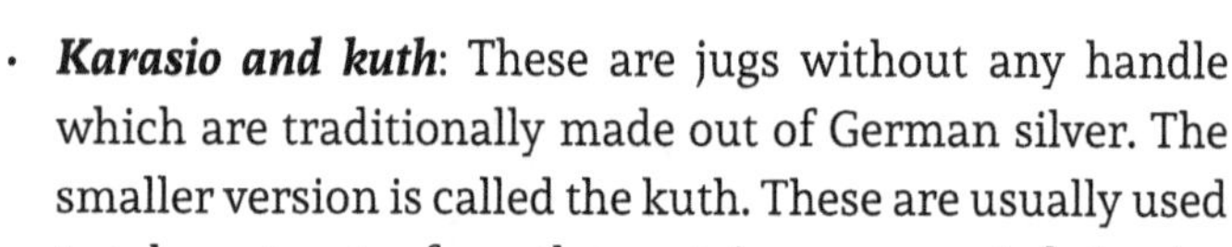

- ***Karasio and kuth***: These are jugs without any handle which are traditionally made out of German silver. The smaller version is called the kuth. These are usually used to take out water from the container or even to bring it.
- ***Boiyu:*** it is alarge colander which is used to drain rice after boiling. It could be used for draining many other things such, but used primarily for rice.
- ***Tapeli:*** these are pans of various shapes and sizes used for cooking food. The shape of a tapeli almost resembles handi or patila used in other parts of India.
- ***Patio:*** It is a flat pan with a broad base and wide mouth, usually used for making a dish called patio, and hence the name.

- **Lohri:** it is frying pan which is something between an kadhai and a tawa. It resembles the sauteuse pan used in western cooking and is used for making stir fried dried vegetables.
- **Popatji nu panu**: It is a type of wok that has got 4 – 8 depressions to make a dish called Popatji nu panu that is eaten as tea time snacks. The utensil is made of cast iron and has depressions in which the batter is poured. The dish is placed directly on the heat source and when heated, it is oiled and batter is poured into the depression and cooked on both sides.
- **Sadhna nu vasan**: This is a kind of steamer used for preparing a special dish called sadhna made from rice flour. This vessel is quite similar to an idli vessel. It is filled with water up to the marked level and is kept directly on the heat source. The batter is poured on the perforated tray and is placed inside the container with the lid tightly closed. The steam thus generated cooks the Sadhna.

NINE

SPECIALTIES FROM THE PARSI KITCHEN

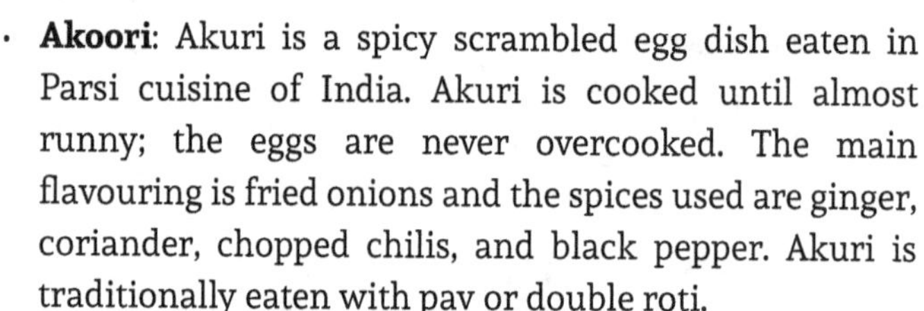

- **Akoori**: Akuri is a spicy scrambled egg dish eaten in Parsi cuisine of India. Akuri is cooked until almost runny; the eggs are never overcooked. The main flavouring is fried onions and the spices used are ginger, coriander, chopped chilis, and black pepper. Akuri is traditionally eaten with pav or double roti.

- **Batero**: This again is a unique dish of meat stewed in toddy vinegar. The meat is marinated with ground spices such as turmeric, chilli, cumin, ginger, garlic, peppercorns and toddy vinegar. The meat is shallow fried in ghee and the rest of the marinade is added to the meat, which is cooked until tender.

- **Chicken farcha**: It's a fried chicken made by the Parsi community of India. It's mildly spiced and then coated in either breadcrumbs or semolina flour, dipped in egg and then deep friend. The highlight of this dish is the mild flavour and the egg coating.

- **Daar ni Pori**: Served at tea – time or as a breakfast treat, Dar ni Pori or Dar ni Poli is basically a pastry filled with a mixture of sweet lentils and dried fruits. Preferably Toor dal is used.

- **Dhan daal patio**: Rice, lentils and fish cooked in a sweet and tangy coconut – based gravy with drumsticks. Dhan (rice), dar (arhar or toor dal) and patio (prawns or fish in a red tomato – based sauce). The dhan is usually plain white or jeera rice. Dar is a simple, creamy dal cooked with turmeric powder and salt.

- **Dhansak**: This is a very famous dish of the Parsis made by cooking lentils with meat, vegetables along with spring onion, mint, fenugreek and coriander.

- **Falooda**: This rose – sweetened milk often combined with ice – cream and corn flour vermicelli. It can also be garnished with soaked basil seeds that swell up like a drop of jelly with a black dot inside.

- **Khimo**: Parsi minced meat preparation. Minced meat of any chicken, lamb, pork, goat meat, or any combination cooked in spices and topped with fried egg.

- **Kolmi no patio**: Curried shrimp in a thickish tangy curry sauce. Usually served with a plain lentil side dish, and rice. It is a blend of tangy, sweet and spicy flavours.

- **Laganshala**: A tasty Parsi stew made with yam, potatoes, capsicum, onions, ginger garlic paste salt and sugar.

- **Laganu custard**: A Parsi community wedding speciality. To prepare this the milk is boiled along with sugar until it is reduced to half. Powdered nutmeg is added for flavour and when the mixture is cool enough, eggs are beaten into it along with dry fruits. This is then baked in a moderate oven, until the top surface is golden brown and the custard is firm.

- **Malai na khaja**: Decadent Parsi sweet. This crispy, flaky sweet stuffed with creamy mawa mixture and immersed in sugar syrup.

- **Malido**: Malido is the essential sweet dish used as an offering at a Jashan. (Parsi /Zoroastrian religious prayer ceremony) Made from semolina, wheat flour, ghee, eggs and sugar and garnished with nuts

- **Mava painda**: It is a type of cake popular in Parsi/Irani bakery made with mawa eggs and flavourings.This cake is an essential part of any type of function in Parsis.

- **Mitthu dahi**: Mithu Dahi or sweet yogurt is made of full fat milk with the addition of sugar, cardamom and nutmeg powder, many Parsis add in a few drops of vanilla as well. It is an integral dish of any Parsi function.

- **Murgh jardaloo**: Chicken cooked with apricots, a very delicious Parsee dish. Boneless cubes of chicken meat cooked in succulent gravy consisting of dried apricot (jardaloo,) red vinegar and sugar along with a blend of mouthwatering Indian spices and aromatics.

- **Papeta per Eeda**: Tomato Pateta Par Eeda is a Parsi – style egg dish where eggs are baked with a tangy tomato sauce and potato slices.

- **Parsi pilau**: Saffron rice, an Indian rice pilaf seasoned with saffron, cardamom, cinnamon, cloves, orange zest, pistachios, and almonds.

- **Patra ni machi**: Patra ni machhi is a Parsi dish in which fish coated in a coconut chutney mixture, wrapped in banana leaf and steamed.

- **Pora**: Parsi Pora is a popular Parsi Omlette, prepared with lot of spices to give an authentic taste. It tastes best, served between two pieces of toasted and buttered bread (white / whole wheat) along with tomato / mango chutney. It is one of the favorite preparations for breakfasts on special occasions, Jamshed Navroz being one of them.

- **Ravo**: Parsi Ravo is a special dessert cooked on weddings, birthday, anniversarys and festivals in Parsi homes. This dessert has many versions, where vermicelli too has been used in some, though I adapted the recipe from here. The Ravo is just like our Sooji ka Halwa.

- **Salli or wafers**: These are essential to the Parsi cuisine. Potatoes are thinly sliced or shredded and then washed several times in water to get rid of the starch. They are then dipped in cold salted water for at least 30 mins and are then drained, dried between towels and deep fat fried until crisp.

- **Sas nu macchi**: Saas ni Macchi is a unique white Parsi – style fish curry, which stands out for its use of an egg – sugar – vinegar mixture, added at the end of the cooking process, to create a curry emulsion with sweet and sour taste.

- **Sooterfeni**: This is dessert made from sugar and looks like thin threads rolled into large circular size. It is flavoured with rose, cardamom and nutmeg. It is garnished by sprinkling rose petals, chopped pistachios and charoli seeds on top.

- **Tareli machi**: Fried Fish

TEN
PARSI FESTIVALS

Jamshedi Navroz (Parsi New Year)

The Parsi New Year, also known as Navroz or Jamshedi Navroz, is celebrated every year to mark the beginning of the new Iranian calendar i.e first day in the Zoroastrian year. Jamshedi Navroz got its name from the legendary King of Persia – Jamshed, who is said to have introduced the solar calculation in the Parsi Calendar. In Persian,

'Nav' means new, and 'Roz' stands for the day, and together it translates to 'new day'. On this day, people greet each other outside the Agiary temple (fire temple) after the ritualistic prayers. Fire is the most important symbol for Parsis. People then greet each other with the customary 'Sal Mubarak'.

Zarthost No Deeso (death anniversary of the prophet Zarathushtra)

This is an important day of remembrance in the Zoroastrian religion. It is a commemoration of the death anniversary of the prophet Zoroaster. It is observed on the 11th day (Khorshed) of the 10th month (Dae). In the seasonal calendar, Zarthost No – Diso falls on December 26.

It is an occasion of remembrance with lectures and discussions held on the life and works of the prophet. Special prayers are recited, and attendance at the fire temple is very high. There is no mourning in the Zoroastrian religion, only remembrance and worship of the Farohars (great soul) of the departed.

Khordad Sal (Khordad Sal is the birth anniversary of Zoroaster)

This is a very crucial event in the calendar of Zoroastrians. Khordad Sal day marks the birth anniversary of Prophet Spitaman Zarathushtra (Zoroaster). Khordad Sal, celebrated at the March 28, is the equivalent of Christmas for Christians, and it is a day of great festivities and celebrations. During the special day, Jashans are recited, large parties are held, large banquets are served, and Parsis (community) come together to commemorate one of the most important, if not the most important date on the Zoroastrian calendar. The day brings together families from far and wide. They pray and eat together as they revel in the festivities.

Pateti (day of repentance and penitence)

Pateti is New Year's eve for orthodox Parsis who follow the Shenshai calendar. The next day, Nowroz, is New Year's Day.The word pateti comes from patet, the Middle Persian word for repentance. Since thePateti as the last day of the year, it is therefore a day for a person to reflect on their thoughts, words and deeds of the previous year and to repent those that were not good. The repentance allows dedicating the New Year to good thoughts words and deeds in a process of ethical growth. On this day the Parsis clean their houses and decorate them. Torans and flowers are used to decorate the entrance of the house and beautiful rangoli patterns are made of birds, flowers, fish or any other design. On this day, Parsi families go and visit other Parsis and exchange gifts and sweets, special food like Patra ni macchi (fish wrapped in banana leaves), sali boti (meat with potato chips), rava and falooda is also prepared. Theyalso visit the Fire Temple to seek blessings from the almighty by lighting incense sticks.

Navjote

The Navjot (or Naozot) ceremony is an ancient sacred ritual of the Zoroastrian community. It is the ceremony through which Zoroastrian children on the threshold of adolescence are initiated into the religion. In preparation of the Navjot, the children spend many hours learning the prayers which are in the ancient Avestan and Pazend languages. On the day of the Navjote, the child is made to wear the Sudreh and Kusti for the first time. The Navjote is held only after the child is at least 7 years old, because after the Navjote the child is responsible for the duty of offering prayers to God and following the religion and customs. The Navjote ceremony is a public declaration of faith and is performed in the presence of relatives and friends.

Gahambars

Gahambars a festival celebrated by Parsi community is marked in honour of Sky, Waters, Earth, Plants, Cattle and Man which are responsible for the creation of the whole world. There are six Gahambars in a year and each of these gahambars spans for five days. The celebrations of Gahambars festival is marked by common feastings, paying tribute to creator of the world, remembering ancestors and general get togethers, so this auspiciousoccasions spreads the message of peace, harmony among all human beings and signifies for Parsis to be attached with traditional roots and their good deeds.

ELEVEN

SIGNATURE DISHES OF PARSI CUISINE

Saas – ni Macchi

Ingredients

- White fish like Tilapia or Pomfret – 1 lb
- Salt and cracked black pepper to season the fish – ¼ tsp
- Chopped onion – ¾ cup
- Garlic cloves – 4 – 5
- Green chili – 1
- Cumin seeds – 1tsp
- Canola oil – 1tbsp
- Rice flour – 1 tbsp
- Salt – 1 tsp

- Egg – 1
- Cider vinegar – ¼ cup
- Sugar – 1tsps
- Cherry tomatoes – 8 – 10
- Chopped gr. Coriander – 1tbsp

Method

- Cut the fish into desired sized pieces and rub salt/ cracked black pepper on them. Leave refrigerated till the curry gets prepared.
- In a mini food blender or food processor, grind together chopped onion, garlic cloves, Serrano pepper/Thai green chili and cumin seeds to a well – ground paste, add a tbsp. of water, if required for grinding the onion.
- In a saucepan, heat canola oil and add the onion mixture to the hot oil. Cook the onion till it turns pinkish brown in color.
- Add rice flour, salt and 3 cups of water; whisk together till you get a smooth curry; let it come to a boil, reduce the flame and cook covered for 10 minutes stirring intermittently.
- In a bowl, whisk the egg, cider vinegar and sugar together, till the ingredients are well beaten. On a low flame, whisk the curry continuously as you slowly drizzle the beaten egg/vinegar/sugar mix into the Saas preparation to create a thick warm emulsion. This stage needs constant whisking, else the egg will poach.
- Cover and let the flavors cook together on a low flame for 5 minutes; add more water if the curry gets too thick at any stage. Check for desired salt, adding more if required.

- Then cook the seasoned fish pieces in the white Saas curry till they're done; fish like tilapia and pomfret take about 5 – 7 minutes to cook.
- Turn off the flame and add cherry tomatoes and chopped cilantro; the tomatoes need to retain their crunch, so don't let them overcook. Keep covered and serve hot with Basmati rice or crusty bread.

Patrani Machchi

Ingredients

- Pomfret fillet – 800 gms
- Malt vinegar – 6 tsp
- Salt – to taste
- Olive oil – 2 tbsp
- Lemons (juiced) – 3
- Banana leaves – to wrap each fillet separately

For the coconut chutney:

- Curd – 1 Cup
- Fresh coconut – ¼ cup
- Coriander leaves – 1 cup
- Green chillies whole – 6
- Garlic – 2 tsp
- Red chilli powder – 1 tsp
- Coriander seeds – ½ tsp
- Cumin seeds – 5 tsp
- Castor sugar – 2 tsp

Method

- Clean and wash fish.
- Sprinkle vinegar and salt, marinate for 30 minutes.
- Trim, wash and wipe banana leaves.
- Prepare chutney with coriander leaves, coconut, green chillies, cumin seeds, garlic, coriander seeds and curd.
- Add salt, lemon juice and red chillie powder.
- Put the fish fillets in the chutney.
- Apply oil to the banana leaves and wrap each piece separately.
- Steam the fish in a steamer or an idli maker for 30 minutes.
- Unwrap the fish, arrange on a platter and serve with lemon wedges.

Murgh Jardaloo

Ingredients

- Oil – ½ cup
- Onions finely chopped – 4
- Ginger – garlic paste – 2 tsp
- Chicken cut into pieces – 1.5 kg
- Fresh tomato purée – 300 ml
- Turmeric powder – ½ tsp
- Chilli powder – 1 1/2 tsp
- Garam masala – 3/4 tsp
- Water – 2 ½ cups
- Sugarcane vinegar – 3 tbsp
- Sugar – 1 tsp
- Jardaloo (soaked and fried apricots) – 16

- Salli (potato straws) – 150gms
- Salt – to taste

Method

- In a broad pan big enough to hold the chicken pieces, heat oil and fry the onions until light brown.
- Add the ginger – garlic paste and fry for a minute.
- Add the chicken and fry for a further 5 – 7 minutes.
- Stir in the tomato purée, salt, turmeric and masalas.
- Add 2 cups water or chicken stock and cook on medium flame for 20 minutes.
- Once the chicken is cooked, check the consistency of the gravy. It should be neither too watery nor too dry.
- Add vinegar, sugar and jardaloos.
- Cook for 3 more minutes.
- Garnish with the salli and serve with chapatis.

Dhan Daal Patio

Ingredients

- Arhar dal – 1 cup
- Turmeric powder – ¼ tsp.
- Water – 2.5 cups
- Chopped garlic – ½ or ⅔ tbsp
- Green chilies – 1no
- Cumin seeds – ½ tsp
- Salt – as required
- Oil – 1 tbsp.
- Thinly sliced onion – 1
- Salt – 1 pinch

- Oil for frying the onion slices – 1 tbsp

Method

- Pick and rinse the arhar dal well, pressure cook with turmeric powder and water.
- Heat 1 tbsp. oil in a small frying pan, add the sliced onions and a pinch of salt anf fry till golden brown and crisp. Keep aside.
- Check the consistency of the dal. The dal should be of semi thick consistency.
- In another small pan, heat 2 tbsp. oil.
- Add the cumin and when it starts to crackle add chopped garlic, green chilies and salt.
- Fry till the garlic gets browned.Stir the tempering for uniform browning
- Pour the tempering mixture in the dal.
- Cover the cooker with the lid and switch off the flame.
- Let the flavors of the tempering infuse in the parsi dal. Stir after 5 minutes.
- Check the seasoning and add more salt if required. Garnish with the fried onions.
- Serve the parsi dal with steamed rice and patio.

Batasa

Ingredients

- Sifted all purpose flour – 4 cups
- Semolina – 1 tbsp
- Baking powder – 3 tsp
- Salt – 1½ tsp

- Soft butter – 1 cup
- Water – 8 tbsp

Method

- In a bowl mix the dry ingredient. Add the softened butter in little pieces. With the tip of your fingers crumble the mixture till it resembles little beads.
- Add the water 1 tbsp at a time until it all comes together. Do not over knead.
- Roll out into a long even sausage on a lightly dusted floured surface. Cut this into 48 – 60 pieces.
- Roll each one very lightly into a ball. Place this on a baking sheet. Preheat the oven to 325F/165C. Cook for 30 minutes. Lower the temperature to 275F/135C and cook for 30 minutes. Now lower the oven temperature to 225F/105C and cook until it cooks and dries from the inside which will be another hour plus.
- Leave to cool and store in an airtight box.

Lagan nu Custard

Ingredients

- Full cream milk – 4 cup
- Nutmeg – 2 dash
- Saffron – as required
- Butter – 2 tbsp.
- Fresh cream – ½ cup
- Green cardamom – 5

- Vanilla essence – ½ tsp
- Egg – 3nos
- Sugar – ¼ cup
- Blanched slivered almonds – ¼ cup
- Walnuts – 1 tsp
- Pistachios – 1 tsp

Method

- To prepare this delicious dessert recipe, boil milk and sugar till the milk is reduced to the half of its actual quantity.
- Add half of the nutmeg, some almonds and vanilla essence to the milk and mix well.
- Once done, keep it aside to cool down.
- Meanwhile, preheat the oven at 180 degrees and grease a baking tray using butter.
- Next, take a bowl and beat the eggs. Add cream and the beaten eggs to the reduced milk mixture.
- Pour this mixture in the greased baking tray, sprinkle the remaining nuts over it and place it in the oven for 30 minutes or till the top turns brown.
- Use a skewer/ toothpick to check if the custard is baked properly. If it comes out clean, it means the custard is done.
- Take out the custard from the oven and let it cool down.
- Transfer it to a serving plate and decorate it with the chopped nuts.
- Slice the custard and serve warm.

Jain Vegetarianism

Jain vegetarianism is practised by the followers of Jain culture and philosophy. It is one of the most rigorous forms of spiritually motivated diet on the Indian subcontinent and beyond. The Jain cuisine is completely lacto-vegetarian and also excludes root and underground vegetables such as potato, garlic, onion etc., to prevent injuring small insects and microorganisms; and also to prevent the entire plant getting uprooted and killed. It is practised by Jain ascetics and lay Jains.

The objections to the eating of meat, fish and eggs are based on the principle of non-violence (ahimsa, figuratively "non-injuring"). Every act by which a person directly or indirectly supports killing or injury is seen as act of violence (himsa), which creates harmful reaction karma. The aim of ahimsa is to prevent the accumulation of such karma. The extent to which this intention is put into effect varies greatly among Hindus, Buddhists and Jains. Jains believe nonviolence is the most essential religious duty for everyone (ahinsā paramo dharmaḥ, a statement often inscribed on Jain temples). It is an indispensable condition for liberation from the cycle of reincarnation, which is the ultimate goal of all Jain activities. Jains share this goal with Hindus and Buddhists, but their approach is particularly rigorous and comprehensive. Their scrupulous and thorough way of applying nonviolence to everyday activities, and especially to food, shapes their entire lives and is the most significant hallmark of Jain identity. A side effect of this strict discipline is the exercise of asceticism, which is strongly encouraged in Jainism for lay people as well as for monks and nuns. Out of the five types of living beings, a householder is forbidden to kill, or destroy, intentionally, all except the lowest (the one sensed, such as vegetables, herbs, cereals, etc., which are endowed with only the sense of touch).

For Jains, vegetarianism is mandatory. In 2021 it was found that 92% of self-identified Jains in India adhered to some type of vegetarian diet and another 5% seem to try to follow a mostly vegetarian diet by abstaining from eating certain kinds of meat and/or abstaining from eating meat on specific days. In the Jain context, Vegetarianism excludes all animal products except dairy products. Food is restricted to that originating from plants, since plants have only one sense ('ekindriya') and are the least developed form of life, and dairy products. Food that contains even the smallest particles of the bodies of dead animals or eggs is unacceptable. Some Jain scholars and activists support veganism, as they believe the modern commercialised production of dairy products involves violence against farm animals. In ancient times, dairy animals were well cared for and not killed. According to Jain texts, a śrāvaka (householder) should not consume the four maha-vigai (the four perversions) – wine, flesh, butter and honey; and the five udumbara fruits (the five udumbara trees are Gular, Anjeera, Banyan, Peepal, and Pakar, all belonging to the fig genus). Lastly, Jains should not consume any foods or drinks that have animal products or animal flesh. A common misconception is that Jains cannot eat animal-shaped foods or products. As long as the foods do not contain animal products or animal flesh, animal shaped foods can be consumed without the fear of committing a sin.

Jains go out of their way so as not to hurt even small insects and other tiny animals, because they believe that harm caused by carelessness is as reprehensible as harm caused by deliberate action. Hence they take great pains to make sure that no minuscule animals are injured by the preparation of their meals and in the process of eating and drinking.

Traditionally Jains have been prohibited from drinking unfiltered water. In the past, when stepwells were used for the water source, the cloth used for filtering was reversed, and some filtered water poured over it to return the organisms to the original body of water. This practice of jivani or bilchavani is no longer possible because of the use of pipes for water supply. Modern Jains may also filter tap water in the traditional fashion and a few continue to follow the filtering process even with commercial mineral or bottled drinking water.

Jains make considerable efforts not to injure plants in everyday life as far as possible. Jains accept such violence only in as much as it is indispensable for human survival, and there are special instructions for preventing unnecessary violence against plants. Strict Jains do not eat root vegetables, such as potatoes, onions, roots and tubers, as they are considered ananthkay. Ananthkay means one body, but containing infinite lives. A root vegetable, such as potato, though from the looks of it is one article, is said to contain infinite lives in it. Also, tiny life forms are injured when the plant is pulled up and because the bulb is seen as a living being, as it is able to sprout. Also, consumption of most root vegetables involves uprooting and killing the entire plant, whereas consumption of most terrestrial vegetables does not kill the plant (it lives on after plucking the vegetables or it was seasonally supposed to wither away anyway). Among Indian Jains, 67% report that they abstain from eating root vegetables. Green vegetables and fruits contain uncountable lives. Dry beans, lentils, cereals, nuts and seeds contain a countable number of lives and their consumption results in the least destruction of life.

Mushrooms, fungi and yeasts are forbidden because they grow in unhygienic environments and may harbour other life forms.

Honey is forbidden, as its collection would amount to violence against the bees.

Jain texts declare that a śrāvaka should not cook or eat at night.

The vegetarian cuisines of some regions of the Indian subcontinent have been strongly influenced by Jainism. These include

- Gujarati Jain cuisine.
- Marwari Jain cuisine of Rajasthan
- Bundelkhandi Jain cuisine of central India
- Agrawal Jain cuisine of Delhi and Uttar Pradesh
- Marathi Jain cuisine of South Maharashtra
- Jain Bunt cuisine of Karnataka
- Kannada Jains cuisine of Karnataka
- Tamil Jains cuisine of Northern Districts of Tamil Nadu.

In India, vegetarian food is considered appropriate for everyone for all occasions. This makes vegetarian restaurants quite popular. Many vegetarian restaurants and Mishtanna sweet-shops – for example, the Ghantewala sweets of Delhi and Jamna Mithya in Sagar – are run by Jains.

Some restaurants in India serve Jain versions of vegetarian dishes that leave out carrots, potatoes, onions and garlic. A few airlines serve Jain vegetarian dishes upon prior request.

According to survey responses of Indian Jains who identified themselves as vegetarians, 92% would be unwilling to eat at a restaurant that isn't exclusively vegetarian and 89% would be unwilling to eat at the home of a friend/acquaintance who isn't a vegetarian as well.

(Source:https://en.wikipedia.org/wiki/ Jain_vegetarianism)

Parsi History In India

<u>*Arrival in the Indian subcontinent:*</u>

According to the Qissa-i Sanjan, the only existing account of the early years of Zoroastrian refugees in India composed at least six centuries after their tentative date of arrival, the first group of immigrants originated from Greater Khorasan. This historical region of Central Asia is in part in northeastern Iran, where it constitutes modern Khorasan Province, part of western/northern Afghanistan, and in part in three Central-Asian republics namely Tajikistan, Turkmenistan and Uzbekistan.

According to the Qissa, the immigrants were granted permission to stay by the local ruler, Jadi Rana, on the condition that they adopt the local language (Gujarati) and that their women adopt local dress (the sari). The refugees accepted the conditions and founded the settlement of Sanjan, which is said to have been named after the city of their origin (Sanjan, near Merv, modern Turkmenistan). This first group was followed by a second group from Greater Khorasan within five years of the first, and this time having religious implements with them (the alat). In addition to these Khorasanis or Kohistanis "mountain folk", as the two initial groups are said to have been initially called, at least one other group is said to have come overland from Sari, Iran

Although the Sanjan group are believed to have been the first permanent settlers, the precise date of their arrival is a matter of conjecture. All estimates are based on the Qissa, which is vague or contradictory with respect to some elapsed periods. Consequently, three possible dates – 716, 765, and 936 – have been proposed as the year of landing, and the disagreement has been the cause of "many an intense battle ... amongst Parsis". Since dates are not specifically mentioned in Parsi texts prior to the 18th century, any date of arrival is perforce a matter of speculation. The importance of the Qissa lies in any case not so much in its reconstruction of events than in its depiction of the Parsis – in the way they have come to view themselves – and in their relationship to the dominant culture. As such, the text plays a crucial role in shaping Parsi identity. But, "even if one comes to the conclusion that the chronicle based on verbal transmission is not more than a legend, it still remains without doubt an extremely informative document for Parsee historiography."

The Sanjan Zoroastrians were certainly not the first Zoroastrians on the subcontinent. Sindh touching Balochistan, the easternmost periphery of the Iranian world, too had once been under coastal administration of the Sasanian Empire (226-651), which consequently maintained outposts there. Even following the loss of Sindh, the Iranians continued to play a major role in the trade links between the east and west. The 9th-century Arab historiographer Al-Masudi briefly notes Zoroastrians with fire temples in al-Hind and in al-Sindh. There is evidence of individual Parsis residing in Sindh in the tenth and twelfth centuries, but the current modern community is thought to date from British arrival in Sindh. Moreover, for the Iranians, the harbours of Gujarat lay on the maritime routes that complemented the overland Silk Road and there were extensive trade relations between the two regions. The contact between Iranians and Indians was already well established even prior to the Common Era, and both the Puranas and the Mahabharata use the term Parasikas to refer to the peoples west of the Indus River.

"Parsi legends regarding their ancestors' migration to India depict a beleaguered band of religious refugees escaping the new rule post the Muslim conquests in order to preserve their ancient faith." However, while Parsi settlements definitely arose along the western coast of the Indian subcontinent following the Arab conquest of Iran, it is not possible to state with certainty that these migrations occurred as a result of religious persecution against Zoroastrians. If the "traditional" 8th century date (as deduced from the Qissa) is considered valid, it must be assumed "that the migration began while Zoroastrianism was still the predominant religion in Iran and economic factors predominated the initial decision to migrate." This would have been particularly the case if – as the Qissa suggests – the first Parsis originally came from the north-east (i.e. Central Asia) and had previously been dependent on Silk Road trade. Even so, in the 17th century, Henry Lord, a chaplain with the English East India Company, noted that the Parsis came to India seeking "liberty of conscience" but simultaneously arrived as "merchantmen bound for the shores of India, in course of trade and merchandise."

Early years:

The Qissa has little to say about the events that followed the establishment of Sanjan, and restricts itself to a brief note on the establishment of the "Fire of Victory" (Middle

Persian: Atash Bahram) at Sanjan and its subsequent move to Navsari. According to Dhalla, the next several centuries were "full of hardships" (sic) before Zoroastrianism "gained a real foothold in India and secured for its adherents some means of livelihood in this new country of their adoption".

Two centuries after their landing, the Parsis began to settle in other parts of Gujarat, which led to "difficulties in defining the limits of priestly jurisdiction." These problems were resolved by 1290 through the division of Gujarat into five panthaks (districts), each under the jurisdiction of one priestly family and their descendants. (Continuing disputes regarding jurisdiction over the Atash Bahram led to the fire being moved to Udvada in 1742, where today jurisdiction is shared in rotation among the five panthak families.)

Inscriptions at the Kanheri Caves near Mumbai suggest that at least until the early 11th century, Middle Persian was still the literary language of the hereditary Zoroastrian priesthood. Nonetheless, aside from the Qissa and the Kanheri inscriptions, there is little evidence of the Parsis until the 12th and 13th century, when "masterly" Sanskrit translations and transcriptions of the Avesta and its commentaries began to be prepared. From these translations Dhalla infers that "religious studies were prosecuted with great zeal at this period" and that the command of Middle Persian and Sanskrit among the clerics "was of a superior order".

From the 13th century to the late 16th century, the Zoroastrian priests of Gujarat sent (in all) twenty-two requests for religious guidance to their co-religionists in Iran, presumably because they considered the Iranian Zoroastrians "better informed on religious matters than themselves, and must have preserved the old-time tradition more faithfully than they themselves did". These transmissions and their replies – assiduously preserved by the community as the rivayats (epistles) – span the years 1478–1766 and deal with both religious and social subjects. From a superficial 21st century point of view, some of these ithoter ("questions") are remarkably trivial – for instance, Rivayat 376: whether ink prepared by a non-Zoroastrian is suitable for copying Avestan language texts – but they provide a discerning insight into the fears and anxieties of the early modern Zoroastrians. Thus, the question of the ink is symptomatic of the fear of assimilation and the loss of identity, a theme that dominates the questions posed and continues to be an issue into the 21st century. So also the question of conversion of Juddins (non-Zoroastrians) to Zoroastrianism, to which the reply (R237, R238) was: acceptable, even meritorious.

Nonetheless, "the precarious condition in which they lived for a considerable period made it impracticable for them to keep up their former proselytizing zeal. The instinctive fear of disintegration and absorption in the vast multitudes among whom they lived created in them a spirit of exclusiveness and a strong desire to preserve the racial characteristics and distinctive features of their community. Living in an atmosphere surcharged with the Hindu caste system, they felt that their own safety lay in encircling their fold by rigid caste barriers". Even so, at some point (possibly shortly after their arrival in India), the Zoroastrians – perhaps determining that the social stratification that they had brought with them was unsustainable in the small community – did away with all but the hereditary priesthood (called the asronih in Sassanid Iran). The remaining estates – the (r)atheshtarih (nobility, soldiers, and civil servants), vastaryoshih (farmers and herdsmen), hutokshih (artisans and labourers) – were folded into an all-comprehensive class today known as the behdini ("followers of daena", for which "good religion" is one translation). This change would have far reaching consequences. For one, it opened the gene pool to some extent since until that time inter-class marriages were exceedingly rare (this would continue to be a problem for the priesthood until the 20th century). For another, it did away with the boundaries along occupational lines, a factor that would endear the Parsis to the 18th- and 19th-century colonial authorities who had little patience for the unpredictable complications of the Hindu caste system (such as when a clerk from one caste would not deal with a clerk from another).

Age of opportunity:

Following the commercial treaty in the early 17th century between Mughal emperor Jahangir and James I of England, the East India Company obtained the exclusive rights to reside and build factories in Surat and other areas. Many Parsis, who until then had been living in farming communities throughout Gujarat, moved to the English-run settlements to take the new jobs offered. In 1668 the English East India Company leased the Seven Islands of Bombay from Charles II of England. The company found the deep harbour on the east coast of the islands to be ideal for setting up their first port in the sub-continent, and in 1687 they transferred their headquarters from Surat to the fledgling settlement. The Parsis followed and soon began to occupy posts of trust in connection with government and public works.

Where literacy had previously been the exclusive domain of the priesthood, in the era of the British Raj, the

British schools in India provided the new Parsi youth with the means not only to learn to read and write but also to be educated in the greater sense of the term and become familiar with the quirks of the British establishment. These capabilities were enormously useful to Parsis since they allowed them to "represent themselves as being like the British," which they did "more diligently and effectively than perhaps any other South Asian community". While the colonial authorities often saw the other Indians "as passive, ignorant, irrational, outwardly submissive but inwardly guileful", the Parsis were seen to have the traits that the authorities tended to ascribe to themselves. Johan Albrecht de Mandelslo (1638) saw them as "diligent", "conscientious", and "skillful" in their mercantile pursuits. Similar observations would be made by Jame Mackintosh, Recorder of Bombay from 1804 to 1811, who noted that "the Parsees are a small remnant of one of the mightiest nations of the ancient world, who, flying from persecution into India, were for many ages lost in obscurity and poverty, till at length they met a just government under which they speedily rose to be one of the most popular mercantile bodies in Asia".

One of these was an enterprising agent named Rustom Maneck. In 1702, Maneck, who had probably already amassed a fortune under the Dutch and Portuguese, was appointed the first broker to the East India Company (acquiring the name "Seth" in the process), and in the following years "he and his Parsi associates widened the occupational and financial horizons of the larger Parsi community". Thus, by the mid-18th century, the brokerage houses of the Bombay Presidency were almost all in Parsi hands. As James Forbes, the Collector of Broach (now Bharuch), would note in his Oriental Memoirs (1770): "many of the principal merchants and owners of ships at Bombay and Surat are Parsees." "Active, robust, prudent and persevering, they now form a very valuable part of the Company's subjects on the western shores of Hindustan where they are highly esteemed". In the 18th century, Parsis with their skills in ship building and trade greatly benefited with trade between India and China. The trade was mainly in timber, silk, cotton and opium. For example Jamsetjee Jejeebhoy acquired most of his wealth through trade in cotton and opium Gradually certain families "acquired wealth and prominence (Sorabji, Modi, Cama, Wadia, Jeejeebhoy, Readymoney, Dadyseth, Petit, Patel, Mehta, Allbless, Tata, etc.), many of which would be noted for their participation in the public life of the city, and for their various educational, industrial, and charitable enterprises.").

Through his largesse, Maneck helped establish the infrastructure that was necessary for the Parsis to set themselves up in Bombay and in doing so "established Bombay as the primary centre of Parsi habitation and work in the 1720s". Following the political and economic isolation of Surat in the 1720s and 1730s that resulted from troubles between the (remnant) Mughal authorities and the increasingly dominant Marathas, a number of Parsi families from Surat migrated to the new city. While in 1700 "fewer than a handful of individuals appear as merchants in any records; by mid-century, Parsis engaged in commerce constituted one of important commercial groups in Bombay". Maneck's generosity is incidentally also the first documented instance of Parsi philanthropy. In 1689, Anglican chaplain John Ovington reported that in Surat the family "assist the poor and are ready to provide for the sustenance and comfort of such as want it. Their universal kindness, either employing such as are ready and able to work, or bestowing a seasonable bounteous charity to such as are infirm and miserable, leave no man destitute of relief, nor suffer a beggar in all their tribe"

In 1728 Rustom's eldest son Naoroz (later Naorojee) founded the Bombay Parsi Panchayet (in the sense of an instrument for self-governance and not in the sense of the trust it is today) to assist newly arriving Parsis in religious, social, legal and financial matters. Using their vast resources, the Maneck Seth family gave their time, energy and not inconsiderable financial resources to the Parsi community, with the result that by the mid-18th century, the Panchayat was the accepted means for Parsis to cope with the exigencies of urban life and the recognized instrument for regulating the affairs of the community. Nonetheless, by 1838 the Panchayat was under attack for impropriety and nepotism. In 1855 the Bombay Times noted that the Panchayat was utterly without the moral or legal authority to enforce its statutes (the Bundobusts or codes of conduct) and the council soon ceased to be considered representative of the community. In the wake of a July 1856 ruling by the Judicial Committee of the Privy Council that it had no jurisdiction over the Parsis in matters of marriage and divorce, the Panchayat was reduced to little more than a Government-recognized "Parsi Matrimonial Court". Although the Panchayat would eventually be reestablished as the administrator of community property, it ultimately ceased to be an instrument for self-governance.

At about the same time as the role of the Panchayat was declining, a number of other institutions arose that would replace the Panchayat's role in contributing to the sense of social cohesiveness that the community desperately sought. By the mid-19th century, the Parsis were keenly aware that their numbers were declining and saw education as a possible solution to the problem. In 1842 Jamsetjee Jejeebhoy established the Parsi Benevolent Fund with the aim of improving, through education, the condition of the impoverished Parsis still living in Surat and its environs. In 1849 the Parsis established their first school (co-educational, which was a novelty at the time, but would soon be split into separate schools for boys and girls) and the education movement quickened. The number of Parsi schools multiplied, but other schools and colleges were also freely attended. Accompanied by better education and social cohesiveness, the community's sense of distinctiveness grew, and in 1854 Dinshaw Maneckji Petit founded the Persian Zoroastrian Amelioration Fund with the aim of improving conditions for his less fortunate co-religionists in Iran. The fund succeeded in convincing a number of Iranian Zoroastrians to emigrate to India (where they are known today as Iranis) and the efforts of its emissary Maneckji Limji Hataria were instrumental in obtaining a remission of the jizya for their co-religionists in 1882.

In the 18th and 19th centuries, the Parsis had emerged as "the foremost people in India in matters educational, industrial, and social. They came in the vanguard of progress, amassed vast fortunes, and munificently gave away large sums in charity". Near the end of the 19th century, the total number of Parsis in colonial India was 85,397, of which 48,507 lived in Bombay, constituting around 6.7% of the total population of the city, according to the 1881 census. This would be the last time that the Parsis would be considered a numerically significant minority in the city.

Nonetheless, the legacy of the 19th century was a sense of self-awareness as a community. The typically Parsi cultural symbols of the 17th and 18th centuries such as language (a Parsi variant of Gujarati), arts, crafts, and sartorial habits developed into Parsi theatre, literature, newspapers, magazines, and schools. The Parsis now ran community medical centres, ambulance corps, Scouting troops, clubs, and Masonic Lodges. They had their own charitable foundations, housing estates, legal institutions, courts, and governance. They were no longer weavers and petty merchants, but now were established and ran banks, mills, heavy industry, shipyards, and shipping companies. Moreover, even while maintaining their own cultural identity they did not fail to recognize themselves as nationally Indian, as Dadabhai Naoroji, the first Asian to occupy a seat in the British Parliament would note: "Whether I am a Hindu, a Mohammedan, a Parsi, a Christian, or of any other creed, I am above all an Indian. Our country is India; our nationality is Indian". While having an outsized role in the Indian independence movement, the majority of Parsis opposed the partition of undivided India.

(Source:https://en.wikipedia.org/wiki/Parsis)

The Author

Dr. Anshumali Pandey is a renowned & reliable name in the field of Education, Hospitality, Tourism and Tribal Food. He is a Teacher and Chef by profession, and also an Author, a Business Auditor, and an avid culinary traveller to the Indian Sub continental hinterlands. Dr. Anshumali Pandey is a Hospitality Educator (PhD) who specialises in Higher Education, Office Administration, Pay roll, HR, Labour Laws, Audit, and Procurement & Tender Process. He is an Author with 73 Publications consisting of 55 Books and 3 short stories.

His contribution and research in the field of Tribal Food, Tribal Tourism, Forest Tourism and Village Tourism in the form of research papers have brought several laurels to him. In 2018 the Ministry of Tourism, Govt of Indian duly recognised all this and awarded him with a National Appreciation certificate and memento.

The books written by **Dr Anshumali Pandey** are essentially a banquet arising from an experience of over 25 years of Professional life and have boiled down to crisp and accurate writing on his favourite subjects. Hospitality Sector champion requires to be a specialist in many fields and Dr Pandey is one of them. His knowledge is evident from the spectrum of subjects which he has chosen for his books so far, which ranges from being a specialist chef, to Master of Human resources, to Education and to love for children, and topped with Spirituality. For more than two decades Dr Pandey has lived with his family in Western India in general and the Tribal belt of the union territory of Dadra & Nagar Haveli in particular. Most of his time is consumed in helping and understanding the Tribal and rural population of the region and writing scholarly articles and books on his vast area of interest.

Books written by the Author are –

1. Theory of Indian Cookery
2. Beauty and Irony of Silvassa Tourism
3. A Short Indian Food Story
4. Be Your Own Guide to Indian Cuisine
5. Cookery Fundamentals
6. History of Indian Food (2 Editions Printed)
7. The Great Indian Story Book for Children
8. Personal Budget: Easy Work Book
9. Online Classes Log Book
10. Dictionary Making Work Book for School Children
11. The Lazy Bed
12. Hindu Dharm (हिन्दू धर्म) (In Hindi Language)
13. Where is my coffee?
14. Your First Job is Never your Last (Volume 1)
15. You are Almost There (Quick Fix Resume and Interview Hacks)
16. Working for the Enemy? - A lesson in Career Management
17. Public Speaking for the Young
18. A Date With Coffee
19. How to be The Best Hotel Front Office Employee
20. Diploma in Food Production, The complete Syllabus
21. Diploma in F&B Service, The Complete Syllabus
22. Diploma in Front Office, The Complete Syllabus
23. The Time to Speak is Now
24. Munshi Premchand (Short Stories in English)
25. The Housekeeping Department, Text Book
26. Hitchhiker's Guide to Trekking in Uttarakhand

27. Uttarakhand, A divine Land for a Reason
28. Bachhon ke liye rochak kahaniyan (बच्चो ं के लिए रोचक कहानियाँ) (In Hindi Language)
29. Basic Communication Skills of English
30. The Basic Office Organisation Book for Start-ups
31. Hospitality HRM
32. Hospitality Marketing
33. Bakery Ingredients and Tools
34. Human Resource Management for Indian Professionals
35. The process of LAWFULLY operating a Hospitality business in India
36. Indian Classical Sweets: History, Tradition and Recipes
37. History of India's Himalayan Cuisine: Classical Cookery of Kashmir, Laddakh, Jammu, Himachal, Lahaul, Spiti, Garhwal, Kumaon.
38. Vindu: Andhra Cuisine (Part 1 of South Indian Trilogy)
39. Saappadu: Tamil Cuisine (Part 2 of South Indian Trilogy)
40. Sadya: Malayali Cuisine (Part 3 of South Indian Trilogy)
41. South Indian Cuisine - The Researcher's Guide Book
42. The Ramayana for Children and other short stories from Indian Mythology
43. Legends of the Tribal Shiva
44. Third Generation Children's Story Book
45. It's Elementary: The Top Nine Adventures from the memoirs of Dr John H Watson
46. UNITY IN DIVERSITY, The foundation of Indian Tourism
47. The Thar Express: Culinary History of Rajasthan and Gujarat
48. Basics of Computerized Accounting
49. Impact (Impact of Globalization on Indian Social Life)
50. Vishnu – The Lord of Amazing Incarnations

Connect with me: anshumali.pandey@gmail.com
https://notionpress.com/author/337004

*Please scan this QR code on your phone to know more
about the latest and complete works of Dr Anshumali Pandey*